in
need of
healing…

if anyone
is listening

Frank Fahey

First published 1999 by
Veritas Publications
7-8 Lower Abbey Street
Dublin 1

ISBN 1 85390 444 9

British Library Cataloguing
in Publication Data.
A catalogue record for
this book is available
from the British Library.

*The author would like
to thank Teresa
who did the typing,
and all those
who encouraged
this publication.*

Design by Bill Bolger
Printed in the Republic of Ireland by Betaprint Ltd, Dublin

Contents

g

Foreword

This booklet addresses a subject that is central to Jubilee 2000 and is at the core of the mission and message of Jesus Christ – reconciliation, healing and forgiveness.

The process of reconciliation is painful but liberating. The great model and source of Christian reconciliation is the suffering and death of Jesus Christ (cf. Col 1:20-22), which achieved its full significance in the resurrection.

There is a never-ending need for reconciliation within the human family because of people's failings, misunderstandings and wrongdoings. That need exists at all levels and in all spheres of society – within families, between families, between groupings of people, between nations and power blocs. There is a need for it in the Church, which through all ages remains a Church of sinners at individual and community levels.

Part of the Church's mission is to mediate Christ's reconciliation to all people. It has a duty therefore to promote reconciliation within its own ranks and to play a part in helping to ease tensions and end divisions in the human family.

The Church brings forgiveness to people – to those who fail to live up to the demands of their Christian lives and to those who have damaged or cut off their own relationship with the life of the Church. Through its baptised members and its ministers, the Church must hold out the hand of friendship and forgiveness to these people, it must help them to know and be open to God's unqualified love and it must mediate God's forgiveness to them, especially through the sacrament of reconciliation.

The Church itself is a community of sinners and so, as community or communities, is in constant need of being reconciled and forgiven. It stands in need of reconciliation with individuals and groups who have been wronged by people who represent or act in the name of the Church, and who therefore have been wronged in some measure by the Church. These wrongdoers owe it to those whom they have hurt to acknowledge their wrongdoing, make any reparation that is due and seek forgiveness. They owe it to the Church too because they have inflicted a wound on the Body of Christ by their wrongdoing.

Since the wrongdoers in these cases misbehaved not just in their own personal capacity but in the exercise of a Church-related function, or by the abuse of their position, the Church, through appropriate ministers, also bears a responsibility to strive to bring about a reconciliation with people wronged in this way. This will involve acknowledging the wrong done, taking some ownership of it, helping to heal the hurt caused and seeking forgiveness.

Forgiveness is an essential part of reconciliation. There are two sides to it: the seeking of forgiveness by the offender(s) and the willingness to forgive on the part of the person(s) offended. The request for forgiveness must come from a sincere acknowledgments that one has wronged the other person and an expression of sincere regret and willingness to heal the hurt. Furthermore, to show their sincerity, those who seek forgiveness from others must first be ready to forgive those who have sinned against them. Those who seek forgiveness on behalf of the Church must smooth what may be a difficult path for those who have been sinned against and are now being asked to forgive.

The case histories presented in Father Frank Fahey's book depict a range of typical grievances that individual Irish Catholics hold against the Church. Each story is a reconstruction of the substance of an actual experience, although modified and changed so as to safeguard the identities of those involved. The hurt felt in each case is attributed to a failure on the part of Church people (individuals or groups) or to wrongs perpetrated by Church people. Anybody reading these experiences will recognise that each of them speaks for other, similar experiences.

Relating the experiences exposes the deep hurt that has been felt in each instance and shows up failure and wrongdoing in the name of the Church. Each case history features a speaker who needs healing, calls for sympathetic listening and cries out for an experience of the love of God coming through the Church. In each one, we can see at least the beginnings of a healing process and reconciliation. Each of them therefore says to others who have experienced offence that their hurts may be healed by revealing the depth of their hurt, seeking to be heard and accepted, and showing an openness to forgive. They call on those who caused offence, and the Church in whose name they acted, to acknowledge the hurt caused, show their genuine regret and do what is needed to bring about healing by being frank in revealing their own problems and sincere in seeking forgiveness.

Some of the experiences show how tangled the whole area of causing and experiencing hurt can be. Some offenders can be 'victims' themselves as well and need to be understood.

Sometimes the Church's duty to be faithful to the truth of the Gospel is perceived as a barrier to reconciliation. In these cases the task of the Church becomes more difficult. But she must never cease to bring the love of God to all who have a grievance against the Church.

This collection is a contribution to the celebration of **Jubilee Year 2000** by the Catholic Church in Ireland. There are many who can identify with the experiences that come to light here. A reflective reading can lead many who have experienced hurt or have caused hurt to take at least the first steps towards healing and reconciliation. This would be one of the special graces of **Jubilee Year 2000**.

✠ Laurence Ryan
Bishop of Kildare and Leighlin
Chairman, Irish Bishops' **Jubilee Year 2000** Committee

Reconciliation

There is a lot of hurt and anger in our society.
Some of that anger and hurt is directed towards the Church.
Some of that anger and hurt is being experienced by the
  Church.
We are a wounded and a wounding people.
But both the wounded and the wounding have their own story.
Perhaps if we listened to each other we would begin to
  understand.
We might learn that very often our hurting is not deliberate.
We might come to accept that we are all wounded creatures
seeking the same goals, failing to fulfil our dreams.
We might see the stranger, the alienated, even the enemy
as part of our own unfulfilled and broken selves.
We might even see them as fellow pilgrims along the way
and as such be prepared to share our resources for the journey
and together struggle home.
But this can only happen if we truly listen to each other,
listen not so much with the head as with the heart,
and in that listening discover a compassionate Christ
who has come to release into our lives the healing power of
  reconciliation.

Pilgrimage

So we have put this exploration
into the structure of a pilgrimage,
where one does not exclude one's fellow travellers from the
    conversation,
even if one had that inclination,
but accepts, invites, tolerates and listens to
each and every fellow pilgrim on the way.
The Millennium is a pause, a sacred moment of reflection
on our journey towards the mystery –
which for the believer is called 'God'
and for the Christian is called 'Father' –
in company with Christ our Brother,
with his community of followers called the Church,
which is the subject of this healing exploration
or pilgrimage.

The Pilgrims

They walked and talked in groups
and they vowed that they would listen,
to the best of their abilities,
to each other's stories,
without interrupting,
or contradicting,
or dismissing
what they were hearing.
And each person in the group
would be given the same opportunity
and the same empathy
as they had given the others.

In the first group there were those
who were hurt by the Church in
its dealing with unmarried mothers
and 'orphan' children.

A 'fallen' woman tells her story

Why, oh why,
did you denounce me from the altar
and tell the community to have nothing to do with me?
Nothing!
Because I was going to have a baby,
a baby outside the structure of marriage.
Oh yes! You denounced the father too,
whoever the 'sleeveen' was that got me 'into trouble'.
But me, I had disgraced my family
and the good name of the place
– and all this from the altar.
Why? Why? Why?
And I have to thank Sr Emmanuel
who, that very day my name was named
that my baby should not have a name,
walked up the village with the shopping bags,
in full view of all behind the squinting windows,
and straight into my house,
my house of shame,
and shared her love and compassion
with the village 'hoor'.

The parish priest tells his story

The shame, yes the shame,
is not yours but mine now.
There was nothing 'Gospel' in my words,
nothing of the compassion of the Lord I served,
in the harsh, bitter condemnation
of the letter I read out
from the bishop.
It was the standard letter.
I had it for three weeks before I read it,
the standard letter that had to be read out at Mass,
at Mass of all places,
condemning the 'one who got herself in trouble'.
Sr Emmanuel walking up the street
with her two shopping bags
had more Christian charity in her little finger
than all the bishops or I had in our ample girths.
Henceforth, if you remember, but you don't,
whenever the standard letter had to be read out
I got the men in the gallery to stamp their feet
so that nobody could hear what I said
and nobody could write to the bishop
and say that I had neglected my duty
and hadn't read the letter of condemnation
from the altar.

The bishop tells his story

Sitting in my ivory tower,
seeing the plight of so many of these women,
compelled me to consider
that condemnation was the best way
to eliminate the awful scourge of unmarried mothers.
It was a terrible condemnation, and I felt it.
But what was there to do?
I didn't want a 'Curragh' situation in my diocese
with wanton women living in dykes and bushes
with their offspring in the most appalling conditions.
It was your letter to me,
refusing to read out any more condemnatory letters
(and to which I replied, reminding you of your vow of
    obedience)
that caused me to reconsider my approach.
I contacted the Sisters
and asked them to set up a home
to look after these unfortunate women and their children.
They were reluctant at first.
They were not trained for this.
They had no money
except what they could spare and save and scrape
from those who taught in the national school.
And what would they do with these children
when they were reared
and the stigma and shame still clung to them?
But out of obedience
they said 'yes',
for obedience, they said, was foremost
when a work of charity was required.

The nun tells her story

Mary Ellen was from my own village
but she didn't let on we knew each other.
Her action showed me that was how she wanted it
when I met her in the 'Mother and Child Home' one day.
That's where we went each evening after school
to teach and supervise and play with the children
of these unfortunate girls who had 'got themselves into
   trouble'.
Mary Ellen was some classes behind me in the school at home,
a winsome, almost 'Muire-is-true' girleen from Canabullog.
I asked to be changed over to the orphanage to make it easier
   for her.
I liked teaching and supervising the children of these women,
but the tiredness got to me
and I was irritable with them at times, for which I'm sorry.
The nun in charge was a very good administrator.
She was there all day, every day, with them
– mothers and children.
She was from a big family herself - 14 children
and knew how to deal with them.
She was strict – as her own mother and father had been in
   bringing them up on the little farm
where each of them was too busy with different jobs
to get up to any mischief.
But 14 and 140 are different.

She brought in the same regime to the orphanage:
'The devil finds work for idle hands to do' she said,
and was a strict disciplinarian,
too strict at times, I thought.
But then how could you feed and educate and train them
on just £2 a week each?
Only that we shared our bread with them
and almost all our wages as teachers
they'd not have survived.
As it was, we survived and indeed thrived,
mainly on laughter, joy and a lot of love.
But yes! There was pain,
the pain of not being able to touch some hearts
and to sense that they would never be normal
in society's eyes.

A painful adoption

Father, I blame you for it.
It wasn't as if it happened in the forties.
It happened in the eighties.
I met my daughter yesterday
for the first time since her adoption.
She was so beautiful, so full of life
but she was not mine, she belonged to others.
Why did you make me do it?
I know I came to you in total confusion
when I found myself pregnant.
But why did you counsel adoption?
My sister had a baby five years later
and she kept it and my parents reared it.
I know I was for abortion the first evening
but that was in desperation.
And when you said that if abortion was my decision
you would not help me to procure it,
that, in conscience, you could not condone it;
and you outlined the reasons, medical and moral,
that made you feel that you would be participating in murder,
I know that shocked me into realising that what I was carrying
    was a baby,
and on my way to Dublin, to the Family Planning clinic,
the enormity of the steps I was taking struck me,
and I turned back, realising I had only two choices
– to keep the child or to put it up for adoption.
I still resent that you seemed to counsel me about
the problems and disadvantages if I kept the baby
but never mentioned the trauma and the pain
of giving her up for adoption.
You don't realise, I think, or do you,
the anguish, the loneliness, the depression,
the efforts to escape from the reality of emptiness,
by absorbing myself in marketing, trade, business?
I know when I'd meet you during that period
I'd not want you to mention that dark experience,
until finally the mask slipped and I broke down crying
and said I wanted to see my baby.
And when you arranged that meeting with the adopters
and they introduced me to my child, now aged fifteen,
I came to hate you as much as I grew to love her,
for the empty years you caused me.

In illo tempore

Noreen,
when you came to me in desperation,
telling me you were pregnant,
I sensed your inner hell and shattered dreams.
And when the tears dried up, we outlined, gently,
the three choices that lay before you.
Your immediate choice, abortion, was understandable.
I know that when you asked me to help you procure it
(because at that time it had not been made
politically acceptable and socially obtainable),
I refused, giving you my reasons.
I prayed for you when you took the trip to Dublin,
and if you had gone ahead with that decision
would you ever have met the beautiful child the other day
who caused you to laugh and cry and love again?
But do you not remember, and you know this is true,
when we discussed the choices and I tried to persuade you
that your parents were big enough to accept the situation,
you felt the shock would be the death of your father?
You were the apple of his eye and he had high blood-pressure.
Do you not remember the efforts you made
so that nobody, not even your closest sister,
whom I said would also be understanding,
would ever find out about it?
Do you not remember the efforts we made, successfully,
to get you transferred to the farthest part of the country
so that you would be away when the baby began to show?
Do you remember the alarm I expressed
when you had to come home for a funeral,
and you stated that the corset you were wearing
would do no harm to the growing baby?
I know the climate was not favourable then to keeping your baby,
no more than it is now favourable for adoption,
but even the sisters in the home,
for a full six months after your child was born,
urged and counselled you to keep your options open.
At that time, given the measures of social welfare
and the climate of non-acceptance
and the beautiful child that was nurtured by the adopters,
wasn't your decision, although painful and heroic,
not the best one by your own standards,
the best one for your little girl?

19

An orphan tells his story

I read in the papers
that a boy I knew in the orphanage
is up for murder
and blames his situation
on the orphanage and on his parents.
I didn't miss my parents in the orphanage.
I didn't even know I had a parent
until I grew up, later.
I had many friends there.
O'Reilly – he was different,
not different to us in that we craved love,
for he too wanted to be loved,
but different to us in that,
while we were always trying to please the Matron in charge
so she would love us,
he was trying to displease her,
to test if she really loved him.

He ran away and had to be brought back again.
We couldn't understand. He let himself get caught.
In fact, he went into the Garda Station in Dún Laoghaire
and wanted to know if there was anyone looking for him.
He was warned that if he ran away again
he would be punished
and sent to another orphanage,
one that was very, very strict.
But he ran away again and was brought back again
and was warned again...
We were afraid of O'Reilly – he was strange.
He'd stare at you with blank eyes,
and when we let him play in games
he'd always make a mess of them
and you'd think he wanted to be put out of them.
He lost all his friends.
He was sent to another orphanage.
He said he didn't care.

Nor did anyone care for him,
for his father was a doctor he was told,
and his mother was unmarried,
and they never came to see him.
Nor did anyone.

In the second group
there were those
who experienced the Church
as authoritarian,
not caring,
in its exercise of power.

A student speaks

I felt angry,
disappointed and disillusioned.
Of course at the time
I couldn't name these feelings.
I was only seven.
But that is how I felt when I saw
the local parish priest, a scholar and a saint
(so my parents told us),
give four slaps each
to five boys who he said were 'bold'
because they went out of the yard at playtime
to play football in the adjacent field.
And afterwards, that disillusionment was reinforced
when, at school as a boarder,
the teachers, who were almost all priests,
slapped us with the leather or the cane
for misdemeanour, or poor work,
or for mistakes we made in grammar or in syntax.
Not all of them but many of them did it.
We suppressed our resentment
because we had no other recourse.
Now, sometimes, in the most unexpected places,
a deep resentment and anger surges up within me
against authority that bullies,
and against the Church
when it issues statements and directions (not doctrinal)
without consulting
or listening to the laity and lesser clergy.
And I wonder, if the priests had done less 'battering',
would I still have a 'chip' on my shoulder
and a dark shadow in my heart
and a secret resentment in my soul
against anything authoritarian?

A priest/ teacher speaks

'Spare the rod and spoil the child.'
It was the philosophy of education and formation
that we grew up with, experienced and accepted.
We learned it in the home, in school, in life itself.
Punishment and reward were necessary for discipline,
and corporal punishment was as much a part of life
as eating, sleeping, football or smoking.
There was no other method or model proposed to us.
Of course it was distasteful to ourselves
and very often it was measured and in proportion
to the crime, the breaking of the rule, the situation.
But I know that in the silent moments of my twilight years
I wonder, whenever I meet these lads,
will they speak to me
in a world that has changed
and changed radically,
so that corporal punishment or punitive impositions
are politically incorrect and socially unacceptable.
It pains me deeply when I meet a past pupil
and, part in jest and part in earnest,
my efforts to make them learn or form good habits
by the use of the cane
are alluded to in the company, in my presence,
and I feel like a pariah.
And if I were honest with myself
I too feel disillusion, and shame,
that as a priest, a representative of Christ,
I could not have found another way to make them learn and be
    formed
and not waste their parents' money,
(the money got from selling the needed cow
to put them through college),
except by not sparing the rod
to avoid spoiling the child.

A story of goalposts

It was a simple thing.
A set of goalposts
for the football match at the annual sports
run by us, the Junior Legion.
We had them last year
and returned them safe and sound,
and when we asked you for them again this year
you said 'No'
and we were surprised.
But you said 'No!'
and gave no explanation.
And we were left without goalposts.
And yet you'd come into the Legion meeting
and give grand 'allocutions' and tell stories
about different saints in the calendar,
but about our goalposts – nothing,
and you'd never mention the sports.
As the time for the sports came near
we got three goalposts from here and there,
but we were still missing one post.
So we approached a local farmer
who had a cock of hay in the haggard
with a strong straight pole sticking up the middle
to keep it steady.
The cattle had eaten most of the hay around it,
which was why he had built it round the pole,
– to keep the hay standing.
So we approached him – Junior Legionaries, in short trousers,
to see if he would give us the pole for the goalpost.
And he said straight away ... 'Yes'.
'I'll take the hay and put it in the barn
and I'll drop the pole down to you on Friday
so that you'll have it up by Sunday.'
So we had the sports on Sunday and the football match.
But it was the last.
We all left the Legion after that.
And I never joined any Church organisation
since.

The priest's response

I remember the incident.
No, I didn't give the goalposts.
Why?
To my shame there was no real reason
except my own sinfulness.
I can see it now, of course.
Jealousy that someone else could succeed
without me being at the centre of things.
The year before, you took everything for granted,
or rather you took me for granted
to do this and that and the other,
and then never said thanks to me once,
but thanked this one and that one and the other,
as you wrote the report into the local paper.
It was so childish, laughable of me,
and so tragic too,
although I didn't see it that way at the time.
A thousand different excuses and reasons
came into my mind.
I'll need the poles for confirmation flags next year
and they might get broken.
They weren't returned for two weeks last year
and I saw cattle scratching against them in the field.
They're Church property and hard to come by.
A thousand excuses came into the mind
but it was the heart that was in denial.
I was arrogant, proud, jealous and hurt.
I couldn't see it,
but the children could,
and I didn't understand
that a spiritual director
must also be under a director himself,
for there is an old Irish saying:
'A person without an anamchara
is like a person without a head.'

25

A curate speaks

Twelve years!
Twelve hard years
of pastoral work in a busy town,
called upon day and night
by travellers, parishioners, youth and elderly.
Giving totally.
Totally committed.
Exhausted and fulfilled,
not expecting and not receiving
much affirmation from on top,
the love and loyalty of parishioners
sufficient
to keep going, together with prayer,
that nurtured love of God
through Our Lady.
The bombshell!
'I'm moving you.'
In itself to be expected,
but what was not expected
was the tone and manner.
'You're here long enough,
too long in fact.
Making things difficult for others'
(meaning my parish priest).
'He's not too happy with you,
you're causing dissention,
and I've given you more latitude
than I've given to any other priest
in pastoral work.
So I'm shifting you.'
It was a bombshell!
Not so much the shifting
but the accusations,
the denigration,
the humiliation,
even if it was all true.

26

The bishop
replies

Yes – I remember the morning.
I exploded!
I was under pressure,
built-up pressure, for a long time
from others in the dioceses.
You wouldn't be content
to be an ordinary curate,
doing ordinary curate's duties.
You were always trying something new,
although I have to admit you never neglected
the ordinary.
But you weren't satisfied
unless you were trying some new pastoral initiative,
without asking leave or pardon
from your parish priest or from myself.
Most of these, you know, came to nothing.
I know it was a time of change,
a change many didn't notice.
But you were ahead of yourself
and of everyone.
So, even if you had asked for permission,
we would have advised caution and prudence.
You once said the world was dying of prudence
and that we had to be creative and enterprising
in meeting the new pastoral challenges of our times.
But if that is so,
let us do it all together as a team, a diocese.
No one likes singularity.
That was drummed into us in Maynooth.
We were taught there to conform,
otherwise we would show others up
and they would feel it, and they did.
So all this time talk about you was going on in the diocese,
and you didn't seem to be aware of it,
and you went ahead with your pastoral initiatives
and I tolerated it
and you never seemed to acknowledge that,
even when I had to stand up to criticism for not stopping you.
That morning I exploded
over some 'liturgical extravaganza' you had started.
I was sorry afterwards, but couldn't say so.

A primary teacher speaks

There was an interview.
A matter of course, I was told.
My father and his mother too
had been teaching in the school for years.
The interview would be mere 'window-dressing'.
I first heard the news in Raftery's pub,
when the talk stopped as I went in for fags
and eventually one of the customers said:
'We're sorry you didn't take the job above.
You'd have been great, training the lads.
I suppose you'll be off to Dublin like the rest,
playing for Clanna Gael or Civil Service.'
'We're sorry you didn't take the job.'
At least they didn't know I didn't get it.
At home the post-mortems began in earnest.
My father remained silent, but my mother listed out
the hours and days he had spent in the parish
answering every whim and call of the clergy.
They told his mother and she was silent.
She was hurt and asked if it was the canon or the curate
and when I said it was the curate
she took her coat and went up to the presbytery.
She never said what happened, but on her return she said,
'Maybe 'tis better if you flap your wings, Davy.
There's other places in the world besides Dromainy'.
My father never recovered from the hurt, my mother neither.
He was silent, but she gave out and boycotted the curate.
My father never again went shooting with the canon.
He said he was too old and times were changing.
The curate never gave me an explanation.

28

The curate manager replies

We had spoken of it so often in the seminary
– that when we were ordained and appointed managers of
   schools,
patronage and preference would give way to merit
in our selection and appointment of teachers.
I followed all Department Rules exactly
and the panel selected the five candidates for interview.
No! You weren't chosen at the interview,
and neither then nor now am I at liberty to say 'why',
not to your grandmother
when she came calling that night
or to anyone else.
The rumour that I insisted on Miss Friel
because her boyfriend was supposedly friendly with my brother
was both untrue and mischievous,
as was the suggestion that I was ingratiating myself
with the women's movement by appointing her as principal.
The panel was objective and professional
– perhaps, I see now, too professional.
It would, in retrospect, have been better
to have appointed you, in spite of your lack of experience,
as Miss Friel left our school three years later
when she got married up the midlands,
and by then you were firmly established in Dublin.
The canon made an approach to me before the selection
and I, in my righteousness, said I would not be influenced
by politics or pressures or delegation or old loyalties.
'A new broom must sweep clean in the parish.
Appointments must be made by merit and
there is too much of a legacy in our country
of patronage and parish priests making decisions
   independently.'
I had listened to stories in the pub
of how so-and-so's grandfather was rejected
because he didn't wear the right political colours,
and about the dynasties that ruled the roost for years,
and I didn't realise that I too was being set up in style
by those who bore a grudge against the master at the time,
and didn't want his son to get possession.

Dancing and dancehalls

My mother took the canon's side and was against it.
My father took the Regans' side and was for it.
And that, generally speaking, is how the community divided
regarding the dancehall in the bog beyond Gurteen.
It began when young Regan came home from England
with talk about money to be made from dancehalls there,
for great was the scarcity of men after Somme and Flanders.
The older brother, who had the shop, financed the venture,
and so a dancehall of green galvanise appeared in the bog just below
    Gurteen and all the locals began to flock to it for 'diversion'!
The crunch came when it became all night (until 2 a.m. really!)
and the canon, in the other part of the parish, heard about it.
It was the Somme all over again – all-out war,
the canon hurtling missiles from the pulpit battlement,
the Regan brothers from the trenches behind the counter in Gurteen.
As youngsters, we weren't supposed to know about the 'scandal'
but, pretending to be asleep, we'd hear our parents arguing,
or with cocked ears we'd hear the remarks of the older lads
as they played pitch and toss at the crossroads.
My father said 'twas all about power and money,
my mother said 'twas about decency and morals.
D-Day came on the occasion of the obsequies in Gurteen
of a very important person, whom the relatives deemed
was more worthy of a panegyric from the canon than the local curate.
I was an altar boy that day at the funeral
and the canon was about to launch into the panegyric
when he spied the Regan brothers leaning against the pillar.
The panegyric quickly became a harangue
about dancehalls and agents of the devil
leading men and women down the road to sin and hell.
The canon didn't mention names but everyone applied it,
and he was going on and on in quadraphonic
until suddenly he stopped and realised
that he had still said nothing about the dead.
So, by way of consoling the relatives, I suppose,
that the dead man was out of reach of these temptations,
he turned towards the coffin and proclaimed:
'Well, his dancing days are over, anyway'.
My father no longer argued but laughed heartily,
and eventually the episode became folklore and lost nothing in the tellin
The Regan brothers and a few others continued with the battle
and the families of that very important person
complained to the bishop about the canon.

The canon and dances

I served as a young curate then (the late '20s) under the canon,
and I had to read out, on the first Sunday of each quarter,
the statement from the bishops and archbishops of Ireland
denouncing house dances and crossroads dances and all dances
that weren't properly supervised and chaperoned,
warning the flock about the 'sinful occasions' and dangers
and the 'temptations of the flesh' that all these were,
paths that led innocent girls down the slippery slopes to hell.
It was the canon's Achille's heel, for otherwise he was
    balanced.
Maybe it was something in his youth or ministry
or in his training in France.
'Did you read out the letter?' he'd ask.
'Sure, they know it now by heart,' I'd say.
He let it pass until the dancehall on the other side of the parish
opened its doors, all night, to this debauchery, as he saw it.
The canon got sick – physically sick, genuinely ill.
'The abomination of desolation' in his parish!
Talking was no good, he would hear no argument.
He had the weight of the hierarchy behind him.
It was a sad time really, restricted, fearful and barren.
Sex was for procreation only,
and even within marriage it had no place
for the creation and nurturing of relationships.
Kavanagh puts it well for many situations:
'Like the after-birth of a cow
stretched on the branches in the wind,
life died in the veins,
of these men and women.'
Suppression must have brought a lot of pain and frustration,
although suppression was by no means universal,
as the Canon learned when he accosted Molly a'carting.
'Go home, Canon', she said,
'You don't know what you're missing!'
And these men of the cloth, sincere in their efforts,
must be turning in their graves now, in this age of liberation,
when they see sex used more for recreation than procreation,
with even sadder and more painful consequences,
for neither suppression nor free expression is redemption.
When the canon's own 'dancing days' were over,
the Regan brothers came to his funeral,
although some of their followers remained bitter.

A reflection

'Hosanna!' they shouted, 'Hosanna!' or something like that,
except it wasn't the Son of Mary and Joseph, but Karl Woyola,
and he wasn't coming into Knock on a donkey,
but in a helicopter, and we weren't strewing palms on the road
but corralled in sections of the large field – that year of 1979.
It was a mighty affair – the Church triumphant,
a far cry from the silence that greeted the Mother of God
and her Son the Lamb, with John, Joseph and angels in 1879.
The laity that day were corralled to keep them in their places,
while in the front rows the bishops and priests and dignitaries
sat in serried ranks of various hues and authority.
What happened at Knock was a watershed in the Irish Church,
the day the Pope arrived, or rather left – so suddenly
that he could not go around to visit the corrals,
and people were left dumbfounded, bewildered, disappointed,
after walking and standing and praying and starving for hours.
The eight miles to Claremorris was thronged with people
wearily walking back to where their cars were parked,
and they were angry – angry that only the dignitaries,
both lay and clerical, had got the chance to meet His Holiness,
and they were left without any intimate contact with greatness,
except with Christ, in the Eucharist,
or in the tired weary travellers on the road to Claremorris.
Among those walking was Fr Tom, a priest
who also received the barbs and jibes and smart remarks
from the angry, disappointed, weary crowd.
Those around him felt pity for him; his legs were gone.
James Peter's donkey was looking out a gap,
and he was commissioned by one of the lads
and Fr Tom was put up on his back, grateful for the ride.
And that was the way he rode into Claremorris that evening,
and those before him and behind him and those around him
smiled and joked, not with vilification but with banter.
There was a shared humanity on the same journey.
Fr Tom and the donkey redeemed the day.
It was the road to Emmaus really.
We failed to realise that the Church as institution must suffer
in order to enter its real glory as community.
We had the experience but failed to recognise its meaning,
like the disciples on the road to Emmaus,
until the bread was truly broken
some two decades later.

Then there was
the group of priests and ministries
who felt aggrieved
by attitudes towards their ministry
within the Church.

'A spoilt priest' tells his story

It was the early forties.
For months the agony went on.
I was in Maynooth, mainly because of my mother.
She wanted me to be a priest,
to have something to make her feel
that her life of hardship, pain and prayer had a meaning,
that God loved and blessed her in this way,
by having a priest in the family.
After a few months the doubts came.
I prayed, I was obedient, I studied,
and yet the doubts would surface.
But how could I leave,
bringing heartbreak to my mother
and shame to my father at the fair,
where he was so proud to talk about me
to the other farmers and jobbers
when they would laugh and joke and pull his leg:
'How in the name of God could you have a son a priest
and all the hoofling and tangling and bargaining you do!'
And if I did leave, would he blame himself,
for something he did or did not do,
that God rejected me?
'The spoilt priest.'
That was the name I'd be given,
as it was given to Philip Mongan and stuck with him
all his life when we were youngsters.
'The spoilt priest' – a kind of creature
born out of time and place,
blighted in some way with traces of Judas.
I left but didn't return home;
the pain would have been too much
for mother, father, family and some neighbours.
There would be the few
for whom I would be the source of gossip,
and others, if I failed in anything,
who would have the ready answer:
'He's a spoilt priest, you know'.

I left for England and told my parents
I'd be writing later.
And Mother Church,
you never claimed me as your own,
yet I was faithful.

A married 'priest' tells his story

We have been too quiet.
We left quietly
and have lived quietly,
when we should have been shouting from the rooftops
that it is all wrong, all wrong.
To think that human love is wrong,
to think that human love is deemed so wrong
as to prevent us from serving God
in priesthood.
Who made these laws and why?
Why?
For fear our sons would take control?
For fear our daughters would inherit?
For fear we wouldn't have enough love
for others
if we loved our family too well?
But love begets love
and love is tested
in close relationships,
and must grow or die.
In marriage there is no room for disengaging,
no time for crabbed bachelorhood,
no time for cranky priests,
for we must grow in love or die.
But why, oh why,
just tell me why
is human love
an obstacle to priesthood?
And with all my training
can I not be trusted to take up
a post of administration within the diocese,
or even one of ministry?

35

A conservative priest speaks

You say,
not openly but by implication,
that I am a bit of a fanatic,
that my devotion to Our Lady,
my enthusiasm for pro-life and marriage
are a bit too much for you to handle.
You come across to me
as cool about it,
taking a reasonable middle ground
between the liberals and conservatives.
In all matters one must be
politically correct,
in Church as well as in secular circles.
Being politically correct
in Church circles
is important, isn't it?
I know it is,
for I have been told
by my clerical friends
that if I want to advance
(they say I have a big future)
then I must be moderate in all things,
like divorce, pro-life, family planning, devotions.
This hurts.
You can be enthusiastic about golf
and talk about handicaps and tournaments,
or about a school or church you are building,
or about anything other than principles.
It is important to say the right thing
when interviewed on Radio and TV,
to be for married priests
and women priests,
the environment,
optional celibacy,
democratisation of the Church,
a 'with it' Pope,
more sensitive bishops,
more authority for the laity –
following the politically correct agenda
set in clerical gatherings
after the official meetings.

A liberal priest speaks

Running on railway tracks,
no scope to turn aside, explore, encompass,
the sacraments at every station
and every station a sacrament,
train-drivers trained to keep the trains on track,
signal-men to decide when to shunt and who to move.
Is that the kind of Church that will electrify the future?
Rath Brazil and Kells in the twelfth and thirteenth centuries
were significant happenings in the Irish Church,
and changed around the barque of Peter,
only for it to settle down again, in a few centuries
to become a tanker, a monolithic tanker
that can only move in one direction
and needs miles and miles of ocean to make a turn.
I would prefer, as a liberal, to imagine the Church
as a hovercraft rather than as the barque of Peter,
for the hovercraft is free to move in many directions.
I am against a one-track Church,
where everything and everyone must conform,
a sort of psychological doxology
'as it was in the beginning
is now and ever shall be',
as if the way things are now
is the way they always were and always will be.
The Church had to change or die in the twelfth and thirteenth
    centuries.
Today it is obvious to all that we need a sea change
to engender enthusiasm and involvement again,
to get a tired, jaded Church up and moving.
You may ask me – what is it we need?
Can you not see? It's as plain as your face!
A married priesthood and women priests,
lay involvement with real authority.
There is only one way forward.

37

The lay ministry

There were no grants this year.
The diocese, we were told, had decided
that there would be no further grants
for theology students or training of catechists
or for spiritual, liturgical or pastoral courses,
unless the recipients were clerics.
What is the message we are receiving?

And when, out of our own pockets,
we did the courses for these particular ministries,
we felt we were second-class citizens of the Church,
accepted only to fill the seats left vacant
by the diminishing number of clerics.
What is the message we are receiving?

And when we have to study in cramped conditions,
yet see large institutions in the diocese vacant.
What is the message we are receiving?

And in a diocese where there is clerical scarcity
and half-parishes stand empty of a priest's presence,
could they not be partly served by a duly appointed lay
   minister
who would be financed out of the priests' collections?
I understand that this is not acceptable.
What is the message we are receiving?

Is it that, as teachers of theology
or liturgical animators,
pastoral strategists or prayer leaders,
parish catechists or scripture sharers,
a lay person in these ministries
is not equal, really,
to the person with clerical status
who is performing the same ministry?

A new springtime

Ní mar síltear, bítear.
Things are not what they seem.
The cost of educating our clerical students
has become so exorbitant
that there is no money left in the diocesan coffers
to grant-aid any of these other courses,
as some other dioceses do.

If the message received was different
we apologise and say sorry.
We are trying to do something about the situation.

If there were no rooms available in diocesan institutions
to provide appropriate accommodation for lay students,
that was because the conditions of our constitution
and the express wishes of our benefactors
prohibit it.

If the message received was different
we apologise and say sorry.
We are trying to do something about the situation.

If you felt you were merely tolerated as second-class citizens
as you pursued your course with clerical students,
and if you were aggrieved with the diocesan decision
not to use the revenue from the 'priests' collections'
to support a lay minister in a vacant half-parish,
there may be some validity in your assertion.

It is true that we have still not fully accepted
your right, as a baptised person,
to exercise these specific ministries in the Church,
and with that right comes the grace of vocation
and our obligation to assist in its fulfilment.

It will take time for us,
not just bishops and priests,
but other lay people too,
to accept and welcome this new 'springtime',
and to give moral and financial support
to fulfil it.

A celibate priest tells his story

It wasn't so much the fact of celibacy,
but how it wasn't or isn't appreciated by the laity,
those whom primarily it was meant to serve,
that hurt most.
In the early days in Maynooth
there was the struggle to accept
that the natural and human desires
to form deep relationships with 'the opposite sex'
could not be consummated in marriage
if one were to be called to priesthood.
But through prayer, reflection and grace,
one finally grasped its appropriateness to priesthood,
to serving the people with a celibate love
that was inclusive, unconditional and creative
and by that way of life
to be a sign of the resurrection
in the Kingdom already present but not, as yet, completed.
On Ordination Day the die was cast,
and the irrevocable decision was made to accept the charism
and by God's grace to keep resolutely the commitment given.
But it wasn't so much the fact of celibacy that hurt
as the lack of appreciation by the community
that had been served with an inclusive love for thirty years.
And I was hurt when, on the local radio programme on celibacy
you, of all the couples that had required so much of my time,
said that priests should be married,
and that you didn't see any advantages to celibacy.
And the studio audience were of the same opinion.
And I thought of the lonely nights and moments when
I comforted myself with the presumption that my sacrifice
(perhaps not heroic but at times bordering on that)
was appreciated and its sign of the Kingdom accepted.
And it wasn't until long into the night, before the Blessed
    Sacrament,
that I realised and recalled what had been the decisive element
    in the choice,
namely, that celibacy, like martyrdom and heroic marriages,
is first of all the living out of what is deepest in the heart,
of one's own fierce conviction of the resurrection and its
    implications,
and then, for those who are faith-gifted and open,
it can be a sign of the same conviction.

d

The next group
was the most vociferous,
and felt the pain of pilgrimage
most acutely –
those caught in sex abuse
and scandals.

A paedophile tells his story

At the Penance Service I confessed I was a paedophile,
and as you gave me an anonymous absolution
I whispered:
'Father, I need help, desperately'.
You told me to call round to the presbytery.
Some days later I got the courage and went
and I told you my story.
How it all began when I was six
in an act of sex, initiated by a grown-up woman.
I told of how, from that time onward,
I was plagued, possessed (you said obsessed)
by some inner compulsion
to expose myself to children.
I lost restraint mostly when I had drink taken.
I noticed your slight unease, but you were silent
and you didn't say straight away:
'Three Hail Marys and avoid occasions'.
I told you that I had already tried to cure it.
A holy man in Cornwall – but it didn't work.
A quack in Northern Ireland – no better.
Once in desperation I took hold of a live electric wire
and asked God for the shock either to kill or cure me,
for I didn't mind, but it did neither.
You asked me did I ever go to a psychiatrist,
and when I said 'no'
you offered to make enquiries to find one,
if I called back in two weeks' time.
In the meantime, to frighten me I think,
you said you thought that the sin was also a crime
and I could land in jail if I was found out.
That was the first I knew about that side of it.
You said the sacraments would help me,
and to be sure and come back again,
which I did, and again and again.
But I'm imprisoned still by my compulsions
and I know it's only a matter of time
'til I'm arrested.
So much for religion!

The confessor tells his story

Now that you have given permission,
I can tell my side of the story.
Yes! I was shocked by what you told me,
for there was nothing about this in our moral treatises.
I asked the local doctor about it and he
thought it was work for a psychotherapist,
although he'd heard there were pills that could lower the libidum.
The psychiatrist said they had barely touched on this in training,
but he imagined that it could be cured by treatment,
and he thought there was a place in England
that dealt with this kind of condition.
When you came back after two weeks
he still hadn't got the address for me.
I was sorry to have to disappoint you,
especially since you further described the awful moments
when, in bed at night, you'd feel a dark weight or cloud
come down on top of you and almost suffocate you
and you felt you were possessed.
I became somewhat frightened and asked in the diocese
who was the official 'exorcist', and was told
that modern thinking said that most 'possessions' were in fact
   'obsessions'
and that counselling and perhaps prayer would be sufficient.
I read a prayer over you that priests use in the missions
when people have been exposed to evil for a long period,
and they become obsessed and drawn towards black magic.
We called on Michael and the guardian angels to defend you,
and I said I would anoint you
if you did a novena of prayer and fasting.
Do you remember the night I anointed you on the forehead,
in the name of the Trinity, and you felt
as if a hot current passed down your body
and healed you in the Spirit,
until you took the first drink again?
And eventually you went to that place in England,
and they sent you home and said
that you could maintain sexual sobriety
if you attained alcoholic sobriety.
But you said you couldn't do the latter.
And I know you're still in prison,
in fact in two prisons,
without even being arrested.

43

From
Arbour Hill

I sit in my cell in Arbour Hill,
totally demoralised and feeling abandoned
by a Church that is supposed to embrace
the greatest sinner.

I was a priest.
I am a child abuser.
The very name is abhorrent to me.
It will always stay with me,
and follow me outside,
no matter where I hide
or try to hide.

It is my release in two months' time
that I most dread.
Where will I go?
Who will have me?
No echoes of the Gospel's care for the 'unclean'
reach me.

Friends, former parishioners, family
will surely shun me.
I will be without friends,
a fugitive on the earth,
the mark of Cain on my forehead
or posted on my door by neighbours.
And there will be no escaping or compassion.
My bishop tells me he is laicising me,
that the Church cannot take responsibility for my future
    actions.
I have cost them so much already.
To say that I am sorry will evoke little sympathy.
Compensation, litigation, awards,
this will be the stuff of years and years to come.
I committed a crime for which there is no pardon.
If I dared give an excuse the media would castigate me.
'Priest Looks for Sympathy after Litany of Abuse.'
I can only apologise and hope
that God will be more merciful than the Gospel:
'Whoever scandalises one of these little ones
would be better to have a millstone tied around his neck
and be cast into the depths of the sea'.

The bishop listens

I do not ask for your sympathy.
I have told no one my story.
I thought I never would,
certainly not the child in me.
It was our secret.
I was the 'apple of his eye'
and I got sweets and chocolate
every time we petted
as a sign that our friendship was special.
It made up for the loneliness
that adults feel, I was told.

I never told anyone in the seminary,
not even my confessor.
The child within me was loyal.
The teenager was ashamed.
The adult I never became, sexually,
was confused.

I knew that if I did tell someone
I would have received sympathy, compassion,
but it would have meant devastation in the family
and I couldn't bear that and the end of priesthood.
I never betrayed the secret,
not even when you sent me for therapy,
and they told you I was cured
and I could be let back to the ministry.
I wanted to be loyal
and I felt that the children I molested
would be loyal to a child's secret,
as I was loyal to mine.
I feel relieved now that they have spoken.
I feel betrayed of course,
but now they can be treated and the cycle broken.
It would be different if I, as a child, had spoken.
But then how could I have betrayed my uncle?

45

Father of victim speaks

I am the father of a victim, an innocent victim,
and I am angry – very angry – with many people.
But that anger seems now to be channelled towards the
   bishops.
They must have known this was going on, but did nothing!
They sent these priests away for treatment, didn't they, but
   they did nothing!
They let those priests back into parish duty, didn't they?
They did nothing to stop this happening, did they?
I am angry, very angry.
No, I don't want to hear about compassion.
I don't want to hear about sorrow and forgiveness.
The life of my child is ruined.
I trusted that priest with my family.
My wife made meals for him.
We gave him our car when his was being mended,
to take kids for a drive he'd say.
Don't remind me.
I am angry.
Did the bbishop come to see us? No!
Did the bishop write to say sorry? No!
Did the bishop punish the priest in question? No!
It took a court of law to do that.
Compassion! Compassion my arse!
These fellows should be castrated.
Yes, I mean that.
Of course, if it wasn't for psychological castration – celibacy,
none of this would have happened.
That's what I pick up from the media.
Yes, I am angry.
There will be no forgiveness,
not even if the bishop comes begging.
He should have been watchful of his priests.
Maybe I also should have been watchful
of my own family.
But I trusted.

46

The bishop replies

You say you are angry. I know what anger is.
I am glad that you can express that anger.
I too am angry,
although it is not politically correct
in clerical or political or media circles
to admit that I have anger within me.
I have anger especially against those priests who deceived us.
They led us up the garden path,
exploiting the trust, in denial of the damage they did,
even when the diocesan commission confronted them.
As far as I am concerned, at this moment,
they shall be laicised whether they wish it or not.
I am angry, although again it's not politically correct to say so,
against my fellow bishops, former bishops,
for landing us in this spot.
Most of what has happened was before my time
and I am landed with their legacy.
I am angry with those experts from the US
who came over and told us, before it all transpired,
how to deal with the situation when it would occur,
as it did in the US, Australia, Canada, etc.
Leave it to the lawyers, they said.
One careless word, one admission of guilt, one apology
could cost the diocese millions.
They never said that there were greater losses than money,
things that money cannot buy – integrity and trust.
I am angry with the psychiatrists and experts
who told me that 'X' was cured
and could be let back to the ministry again.
I know that they knew very little about the condition then
and I'm not angry with them for that,
but for their silence now about their wrong direction,
letting us bishops takes the blame for the ignorance.
I am angry with myself but I cannot express it.
I am angry that these children were exploited.
But I cannot say so to the press or media,
as I would be accused of crocodile tears.
Maybe some day my anger will turn to understanding
for the priests, the bishops, the experts,
when we all learn more about this condition.
But at the moment I am angry,
and that anger is sapping all my energy.

A victim tells
of his anger

I watched you in the courtroom,
and my loathing grew.
You were so calm,
you, the cause of all my troubles:
my attempts at suicide,
the black depression,
sexual problems,
broken relationships,
moving from job to job,
the aggression,
the fear,
the drinking
– the litany goes on....
Do you wonder that I loathe you?
You are the cause of all my problems.

I do not want an answer
nor your f...ing excuses.
Four f...ing years
that's what you got today.
Four f...ing years,
and I got a life sentence from you.

The papers said we were both in pain.
Where lies your pain
compared with mine?
I both loathe and hate you.

A perpetrator speaks

What is my pain?

Guilt that your pain
may go on forever;
hurt that you
will not forgive me;
remorse for the pain I brought to you,
to my family and friends;
despair at not being able to redeem myself
in the eyes of anyone;
depression because
I cannot forgive myself;
anger with God who knew all this would happen,
and knew the consequences of my failure
in my vocation.
That is my pain.
O God,
be merciful to me,
a sinner.

A story from Letterfrack

We taunted him behind his back
and stared him in the face.
He was weak, a 'sop'.
We got him crying one day in class.
We knew he was an easy target after that.

Brother H. heard about it
and leathered us all,
strap on backside,
but we laughed:
he'd not make us cry or break us.
We were too tough for him,
the swine…
I hated Letterfrack
and everything about it.
I'd always hated school
– that's why I mitched
and was sent there.
My father was on the 'batter',
my mother on the 'make'.
'Twas predicted I'd turn out a 'rake'.
But I didn't.
I got tough and formed a gang.
While Brother H. was enemy Number 1,
Brother J. was our prime target.
We didn't manage to break Brother H.
We broke Brother J.
he had a nervous breakdown.
Before that we drove him daft in class,
with him usually chasing us around the room
with a broom.
One day we turned the broom on him.
We couldn't be expelled,
for there was nowhere worse to send us
than Letterfrack.
That was in the fifties.
I heard Brother J. (as he was then)
is up in court for 'you know what'.
We never knew he had his pets.

Brother J. (formerly) speaks

It was a disaster from the start,
being sent to Letterfrack
as a young brother.
I tried to be nice to them,
to be reasonable,
to tell them about Mary
and their guardians angels,
but they'd laugh.

I'd get annoyed in class.
They seemed to like that.
I'd try to ignore them
but they'd never let up –
a little squeak from the front seat,
a fart from the back
and tittering and laughter in between.
Someone would open the window,
others held their noses.
I'd ask what all this nonsense was about,
and I'd hear the whisper
'The pig never smells his own'.

I prayed all the more,
staying up at night beside the Cross;
I thought I understood what Calvary was.
Little did I know.
I shut out the pain, stifled every emotion,
became stoic, indifferent to feelings.
The will would carry on, would carry on.
Then one night while in bed
Joseph came,
a shy boy from a broken home
who should never have been orphaned there.
He was crying for his mother,
and remembered former years, he said,
when he'd creep into bed with her and find comfort.
He crept into mine.
That was the 1950s – and I left the Brothers in the sixties.
But since the eighties I've been waiting
for the knock, the summons, the charges.
It came yesterday.
Now I shall know Calvary.

A cynic in need of help

I am a pilgrim, a cynic, in need of healing.
'We need someone for Letterfrack', the superior informed me.
Not just a disciplinarian but an educator.'
For me it became a challenge and then a privilege.
For some of my confrères there, it was punishment and prison.
We were the policemen of the nation's delinquents.
Not all the boys were bad, just a handful – 'the element'
– as individuals tolerable, showing traces of humanity,
but, as a group, an 'element', disastrous.
I tried the theories of the educational dons – Behaviourism.
But the 'element' were no Pavlov's dogs or laboratory rats
who could be conditioned, by reward and loss of favour.
In them, original sinfulness was deeply rooted,
and unmade in God's likeness we can be diabolical.
The previous regime, my Superior said, was too oppressive,
coming from the oppression of bad theology,
where God was seen more as policeman than as Father.
Vatican II's theology of unconditional love was the ideal.
But that kind of love brought about the crucifixion,
and that's what the 'element' did to some of the Brothers.
I remember the morning I 'blew it'.
We had just painted the recreation hall pink,
with money I got from my brother at Christmas,
and on it was scrawled, in black writing:
'Beware the pink panthers you black bastards'.
I called out the leader of the 'element' in front of the assembly.
There under his nails the black paint was still embedded.
I waded into him. He smiled. I lost it.
Christ, you were patient to the end and were victorious.

My guilt turned to cynicism and anger and grows each day
when I see the services now available for the 'elements',
and the amount of money spent on their 'reformation'.
And I think of my mother and so many of her generation,
living in the prison of their homes, behind locked doors,
afraid of being robbed, raped or murdered
by the juvenile delinquents who roam the streets at night,
and the nightly chorus on the TV and radio of those
who wash their hands of past and present.
I am part of this pilgrimage, a cynic in need of healing,
if anyone is listening.

This group
were mainly women
who felt inferior
in a male-dominated Church.

A woman's 'churching'

Deep down I feel resentment against the Church
and it surfaces in the most unlikely places.
Its seed was sown when I observed my mother
being 'churched' after Mass one day.
She was after having my baby brother,
and on her first Sunday back at Mass
I was sent around to the sacristy
to ask the priest to 'church' my mother.
I, of course, being inquisitive, asked why and what and how,
and the information was duly supplied next day
by the senior girls in the national school, who said
that after having a child a woman is deemed unclean,
and she must get a blessing in order to be clean.
Was there something wrong with childbirth then?
Was it unclean, dirty, wrong, sinful?
Were women who had babies in their wombs
sinful and dirty, unlike Mary,
because 'blessed was the fruit of her womb'?
And was that why we couldn't be altar servers,
not that we ever dared to ask,
because that was the task of boys, and that was that.
And if, in company, a woman priest was mentioned,
my mother and all her friends would laugh
and say 'Now that's the job for Mrs so-and-so,
she was always heading for the altar.
Imagine her a priest and having to go to her
for confession!'
Even women put women down in those days,
for we were reared and formed and told
to have a lowly opinion of ourselves.
'Behold the handmaid of the Lord'
was to be the pattern of our service.

It wasn't that all priests were intolerant,
but that they felt we women were dangerous.
And yet they could be kind and very human,
and showed feelings and deep emotion
if tragedy or death or pain came to the family.

A priest replies

Yes, we were neurotic, many of us,
neurotic about sex and women.
In fact, sex was taboo.
Perhaps it was the influence of Jansenism,
which had invaded Maynooth in its early days,
when all the professors had been trained in France,
the home of Jansenism,
which held that sex was somehow sinful.
We neither knew ourselves and our own sexuality,
much less understood the same in women.
We didn't know how to deal adequately
with the gift God gave people
to propagate the earth and form relationships.
Indeed to 'propagate' was seen to be the only purpose
of the taboo word and activity.
So it is true that there were some
who combed beaches and belted hedges
to stop young couples from 'excessive courting'
and indulging their 'carnal appetites',
which was at the root of all sin and trouble
and had to be suppressed
or if possible eliminated.
And it was expressed at one clerical conference
by a senior cleric
(in the early days when sex and sexuality
became part of in-service training)
that 'with regard to sex there is no cure for it'.
Looking back on those days now, I do so
with much embarrassment and some resentment
that we were given such a narrow concept and training.
Our chastity was heroic but flawed
and it often led to us becoming neurotic.
Suppression of expression was the task given
and therefore we saw women as temptation
who must always be kept at arm's length.
And any feelings we might have had
towards some of these good and lovely creatures
were concealed under a gruff exterior
and expressed, in response to their loyalty,
by allowing them to clean the house
and darn the socks.

Priesthood – a woman speaks

I find it hard to be dispassionate
about the issue.
And the direction from the Vatican
that the matter cannot even be debated
is ridiculous.
Why should our gender be excluded
from God's privileges?
I'll tell you why!
It's not God who does it.
It's the Church –
male-dominated.

I'm angry that we have
no recognition,
no status,
no privileges,
no power,
no authority
within the Church
that Christ founded.
I don't want reasons
for or against women's ordination.
I want equal rights
conferred at Baptism
– the right to ordination.

A curate replies

And just suppose it were to happen
that a woman was ordained
by some unusual bishop
but was given
no recognition,
no status,
no privilege,
no power,
no authority –
much like Christ
on Calvary.
Would you be satisfied
with the situation?
What is it we seek in priesthood really?
I am reminded of a time
when the issue of women priests was being debated,
and a PP-pecked curate whispered to another
(while the PP was holding forth eloquently)
'Don't you think it's time
that some of us curates too
should be ordained?'
What is it you are seeking really?
Is it the wrong debate
we are debating?
Are we debating
ordination to authority
or priesthood?

A woman hurt in a clerical relationship

You came looking for friendship
or companionship or something.
It was exciting. I did not understand celibacy.
It was a challenge and a mystery.
I entered into the relationship,
which I thought had some future.
I was single and insecure;
you were ordained and mature,
and so I thought you knew where it was going.
Then you said: 'It must finish.
We can't afford to see each other.
It's interfering with my work.
It's not in keeping with my priesthood.'
It was a bombshell! How could this happen?
It was rejection. Something died within me.
I started to hate God and Religion.
You, however, went on saying Mass, hearing confessions,
counselling the doubtful, comforting the sorrowful,
while I bore all the wrongs silently,
torn apart by what you called infatuation.
And when I passed your house each day
I was filled with anger and with pain,
especially when I'd see another car, blue,
parked outside your door.
And I thought to myself:
'Foolish woman!
You'll be dumped too!'
Perhaps now, after all these years
you'd give me an explanation.

The priest replies

It wasn't intended. It just happened.
It was an inner awakening and it was beautiful.
But when the relationship became exclusive
I realised that it was not appropriate.
My spiritual director
advised me to finish it abruptly
and to occupy my time and mind
with pastoral engagements, to remember
that I was wedded to the Kingdom.
I knew the pain you must have suffered,
apart from the seeming rejection,
for I too was suffering, dreadfully.
And then there was the psychic loneliness
and the questions:
Why had I not experienced this before ordination?
If I had, would I have gone ahead and taken a vow of celibacy?
I longed for female companionship,
not sexual but intimate, pure intimacy.
How could I continue in the ministry
with this slow process of personal disintegration?
I asked the bishop to move me from the parish.
I couldn't tell him the real reason; the one I gave him was
    inadequate.
So I pretended you never existed, but the more I did,
the more your voice and image and presence persisted,
for the heart is a lonely hunter.
What is purgatory? The jealousy of seeing you with another.
What is hell? To live without one's inner soul,
which you seemed to have stolen, and I thought you evil.
Only in time, after a long inner journey, did I discover
that what you awakened in me, as in a mirror,
was my own female side, my anima, seeking recognition.
If I had recognised that then, I would have handled what
    happened differently.
With grace we might have become soul companions.
I'm sorry, Brigid.

Maybe that too is what the Irish Church, as institution, was lacking.
It ignored its anima.
That anima was embodied in St Brigid, your patron,
the nurturing mother of the early Irish Church,
Muire na nGael.
We're sorry, Brigid.

Limbo – the pain of mothers

I took the spade
(not an appropriate tool for archaeological investigation)
and my father asked me as I was going:
'Where are you off to? Is it to the fort in Lis na Sídhe?'
'Yes,' I said, 'I want to investigate the subterrain'.
'Don't touch the rath around it,' he said, 'It will be unlucky.'
'Why?' said I, 'Do you believe in fairies?'
'No,' he said, 'I'd prefer you didn't touch it.'
Then he came out with the staggering revelation:
'That's where they buried my infant brother'.
Limbo – the graves of unbaptised babies,
their little bodies buried in unconsecrated ground,
their souls shut out forever from the light of heaven.
Such was the Church's teaching.
What anguish it must have brought to mothers,
and to my paternal grandmother.
The fort of Lis na Sídhe and other forts and gardens
was where the fathers brought the little bodies,
entrusting them to the sídh or holy angels,
when Mother Church would not embrace them.
I was within one year of ordination,
and by then the Church's teaching had been altered
about those who died without Baptism.
My grandmother must have known the truth in heaven
long before the Church rediscovered
that God is a merciful Father
and Christ a universal redeemer.
And I thought of all the lonely hours and moments
and the days and nights of anguished sorrow
when these women prayed in hopeless faith
for their unbaptised children.
'Rachel weeping her for children, uncomforted.'
And I wondered would I, too, end up a heartless theologian.

A theologian replies

What answer can we give?
The head has many answers and excuses.
The heart has no answer except:
'Sorry'.
We theologians had read the signs too sharply,
and dissected the Good News thoroughly to discover its
    mystery,
as scientists do today, counting the number of molecules
and analysing the biochemical complexity,
thus explaining all phenomena.
It was an age when angels danced on pinheads
and The Mystery was captured in one Godhead,
two Natures, three Persons, four Relationships and five
    Processions.
We posed questions about the Message and the Mystery
that we could not answer,
and then proposed solutions
that led us up religious cul-de-sacs.
Some say it wasn't Church teaching but theologians.
But people were led to believe in it
and it was the heart that suffered.
I wish we theologians
would be more humble
before the Mystery
and before mothers.

There was a group
for whom various allegations
of hurt and failures
and contradictions
made their pilgrim journey
more difficult.

The media – a priest's viewpoint

I sat at breakfast and through the kitchen window
watched a frightened hare pause for breath, eyes and ears alert
for the slightest noise that would signal his pursuers.
The eight o'clock news was on and I felt like him.
You, the media, were again in pursuit of the Church.
This time it was a priest, tomorrow nuns, brothers, bishops,
and if not in the news, then 'What it says in the papers'
or the news analysis or comments from correspondents
would never miss an opportunity to denigrate the Church.
In a short while I'd walk down to celebrate Mass
and I'd exchange nods and waves and greetings
with the people going to work in their cars,
and feel that each one of them, after listening to the media,
would be saying 'There goes another one of them'.
I'd buy the paper after Mass
and both myself and the shopkeeper would try to ignore
the headlines blazing out on the same theme,
and exchange pleasantries about the day.
Some of my friends, both lay and clerical,
have told me they don't buy the paper any more.
My older colleagues in the priesthood say that in the past
discretion was used by editors in matters of reporting
and the quality of mercy was not strained by not telling.
But nowadays in some sections of the media, mainly national,
you seem to take great delight in highlighting,
the faults and sins and scandals and everything derogatory
of one section of society –
the Catholic Church and its institutions.
I looked out the window again and the hare was gone,
running for shelter towards the bog and wilderness,
as were the other hares, running before the beaters,
hired by the local coursing club for their annual meeting,
where the hares would be taken out, one by one,
and two hounds would be set in hot pursuit after them.
I felt like the hares that morning, with you as the beaters,
converging on us, seeking to trap us
and then taking pleasure
in pursuing us
and tearing us to pieces.

The media – their viewpoint

I have listened to your story and noticed
that you have admitted you were protected in the past
from being reported – mercy and discretion being the values
    mentioned.
As members of the media we, of course, are in a different
    position.
Your role grants pardon and forgiveness,
ours is to project life as it is and was and will be,
and to make comment and analyse what we perceive
to be the wrongdoing and hypocrisy in our society,
and to expose in people's lives that which they try to hide.
This is a very important part of any democracy.
And we are, as you know, bound by the laws of libel,
and you will see, in our columns, apologies to people
whose views or lifestyles have been misrepresented.
We, as managers or owners of the media, do not control
what reporters or feature-writers or programme-managers
    produce.
It is, of course, true that they can be selective
because of certain inclinations and opinions they cultivate,
and it is true that some of them have their own agenda.
But we do try to strike a balance.
I repeat, ours is not the business of mercy
or of granting pardon or preaching redemption.
Ours is to expose the faults, the scandals,
and to make some money in the process.
And it would seem to me, in spite of your protestations,
that the public have an appetite for such projects.
And a coursing meeting, to use your own analogy,
can be both pain and pleasure
depending on the view you want to take.
I suppose, if I were honest, I am defensive.
Yes! some of my colleagues may have an agenda.
We'll see what the reviews say tomorrow about this book,
if indeed it is mentioned.

A person hurt in confession

Finally I went in – I was told he was different.
I was outside the confessional box for forty minutes,
struggling to get the courage to go in, after the bad experience
when I had gone to confession in town the previous Saturday.
I was debating desperately in my mind how I would say it,
hoping that the priest was deaf so he wouldn't hear me,
afraid of what he'd say, afraid of 'being given out to'.
I was looking for a sign from God to show me if it was really
   sinful.
(If the candle high up on the candelabra
fell off before being consumed, it meant no sin.
But it remained firm in its holder to the end.)
And so I eventually went in, trembling.
'Bless me Father for I have sinned!'
'How long?', and I knew by the gruff voice
that he was either cross or tired from all the confessions.
I had picked the wrong box, again, this week.
Then the panic started.
Was I going to tell everything and be scolded,
or just tell the ordinary ones and be damned
for concealing grave sins in the confessional?
I started off with the 'warming-up exercises'
– disobedience, told lies, forgot my prayers,
and then I hesitated.
'Anything else?' – silence!
'Anything else?' – another 'warming-upper'.
'Is that all now?' – silence!
He must have known there was a whopper.
I said it as best I could – confusedly.
'That'll be five Hail Marys', he muttered.
'Excuse me', I said, 'but did you hear me properly?'
'Yes', he said, 'Do you want a scolding or a Rosary?'
'Oh no', I said 'I just thought... from my last confessions....'
And then he said:
'Don't be afraid, my son.
Do your best in your struggle.
God is a God of mercy, not an inquisitor'.
And he did a lot
to undo the harm done
the previous Saturday.

A confessor speaks

We did the tract on confession in the seminary
and discussed hard cases like lawyers,
and our exams consisted of what judgement we would give
on situations where property, sex, tax, wages were concerned:
the number, times, occasions, dispensations, restitutions.
You could give exams on those and mark them.
You couldn't give marks on compassion and mercy,
and so confession, as a Tribunal of Judgement,
came to the fore.
Everyone went to confession at that time,
once a week, regular confessions promoted.
Long hours were spent in the confessional
and the same sins were repeated weekly:
I disobeyed my parents (even if they were dead),
I told lies, I cursed.
We didn't need much training in Canon Law
or tracts on justice or sexuality for these.
Then when the big one came up for judgement
we swung into action:
– how often, how far, how much, how terrible?
It was an inquisition,
testing the purpose of amendment,
and their degree of sorrow
and guilt.
The passion of Christ,
the fires of hell,
the horror of sin,
whatever excited guilt and compunction
and firm purpose of amendment was mentioned.
The journey to heaven was not easy, it was narrow,
and the one to hell was broad and well-travelled.
And wasn't the last Holy Communion called *viaticum*,
the legal term for the money given in the courts of law
for the defended to get to the court of justice.
And when I made my own weekly confession
it was to a God of Justice more than a God of Mercy,
and I was often hurt too by the confessor
and I took it as my penance.

A Religious let down by scandals

I read St Paul
and thought I understood
the scandal of the Cross,
but not this cross,
this scandal.

I feel ashamed to bless myself
passing by a Church,
thinking that someone in the bus might say
'there goes another of them hypocrites'.

I don't wear the veil anymore.
The last time I did was in O'Connell Street.
A gentleman walked behind me
muttering and cursing and blaspheming.
I stopped at Clery's window and looked in,
to let him pass,
and in its reflection I saw him still
and his face was flushed with anger
and with drink
or maybe with the lack of it.
He called the attention of the shoppers
to one of them that 'f... up little children',
alluding to a documentary some night previously.
I then realised that I was the subject
of this cursing, taunting, jeering.
And the shoppers all passed by
and didn't try to stop him.
Mother of God,
I know how you felt on Calvary!
I feel so let down by my fellow religious.

A layperson replies

We too are shattered by allegations made against your
  companions.
I suppose we think that if it was done by the laity
it wouldn't be as shocking.
But to be fair
you never said that you were perfect.
You always preached that all were sinners
in need of Christ's redemption:
bishops, priests, nuns and brothers
as well as us ordinary laity.
It was we who put you on your pedestals
and now the pedestals are gone.
Why do you think we should forsake you?
Was there not always sympathy for the priest who was an
  alcoholic,
and the one who was suspended by the bishop was thought to
have been given a special cure, to make up for his misfortune,
by a merciful God, whom you taught us to call Father.
We need people on pedestals.
We need saints in life –
not those who are 'fierce holy'
but those who can admit their faults and sins
and start all over again,
like ourselves.

Your failure
should not lead us to despair
but hope.
Keep going!

The truth

We climbed the mountain with you
on a cold, clear March day
and you recorded from our lips
what we cherished in our hearts,
namely, the story of our search for Truth,
even from prehistoric times,
involving this sacred mountain – Croagh Patrick.
We couched that search as pilgrimage
and unfolded the Truth, as we had, as a people, discovered it,
with myths and stories and legends
according to the modalities of our culture.
It was to be featured for St Patrick's Day
on national radio
and we eagerly awaited its retelling.
Of course it transmitted what we said,
but not what we meant,
and by implication suggested other intepretations
that changed the context of our thoughts and words.
We were warned of course by colleagues
that we would have no control over the final version,
and that producers could put whatever construction they
    wanted
on what one said, by selective editing,
so that one appeared to say what one didn't say.
We wrote to you after the programme, complaining.
We didn't post the letter because we were warned
that it would be of little use and indeed might cause reaction.
But we do wonder, whenever we hear the news,
or watch TV or listen to documentaries,
are we getting the truth or the half-truth?
For the half-truth is worse than the lie
and far more devastating.
And we should both be serving the same purpose:
communicating the truth as we see it.

The half-truth

What is Truth ?
Did you expect all of the two-hour recording
to be broadcast in a twenty-minute time-slot?
Editing is part of every programme,
every article, every feature in the media.
We have to be selective.
On what basis you might ask?
We have to cater for our audience
just as you cater for your congregations.
We have to keep our tam-ratings.
It's our very livelihood.
We know what our audience wants.
That's our business.
With regard to your recording on the mountain,
we have it on the tape recorder
exactly as you said it.
You accuse us of the half-truth,
of leaving out and being selective.
Do you not deal in the half-truth also?
I don't hear anything about hell now,
or mortal sin, or the devil in your sermons.
All these were the sound-bites of yesterday.
I know we should both be serving the truth,
but are people not more interested
in the half-truth?
Our tam-rating is increasing.
Your congregation is diminishing.

Parents lamenting their lapsed children

'It was Rachel weeping for her children,
refusing to be comforted
because they were no more' (Jeremiah).
I wish I could say that for the Church,
but alas, I do not find it.
We are the parents of teenagers
now grown up to adulthood
without a sign of religion or Christianity in their homes
or in the flat where they cohabit.
They tell us that they have values,
not our values but their own.
But in their homes there is
no picture of the Sacred Heart, no crucifix,
no statue of Our Lady, no Holy Water font,
no mention of Jesus or the saints.
One of them celebrated her wedding in church.
That was the last time she was at Mass,
and she says they will send the children
to a non-denominational school,
so that they can make up their own minds.
It's not that they are bad!
It's just that they have no interest in God
or are not moved by the passion of Jesus
and are not impressed by the doctrine of hell or heaven
and don't believe in original sin,
or indeed any sin or purgatory.
We lie awake sometimes at night
recalling the questions we heard in Catechism:
'Those who die in mortal sin
go to hell for all eternity'
or 'Unless you eat His flesh and drink His Blood
you will not have life in you'
or 'He who believes in Him will be saved,
he who does not believe in Him will be condemned',
and all the other things taught us by the Church,
which we lived by all our lives and still believe in.
When we think of the Scripture passage from Jeremiah above
we do not find the Church
weeping for her children, whom she baptised,
or refusing to be comforted because they are no more,
or feeling the pain of parenthood,
although she calls herself Mother.

The Church replies

I put oil on his forehead
and whispered the act of contrition in his ear
and I watched a young mangled body in a mangled car
being kept alive by paramedics
while the fire brigade with giant scissors and cutters
tried to salvage a life from the wreckage
– and I pondered your question!
Does the Church really make the same effort
to salvage life, eternal life, from the spiritual wreckage
that is so prevalent today among the young?
The AA puts up warning signs:
'Speed Kills'.
Do we, the Church, do the same in a spiritual sense?
The Government puts up bill boards
'Don't drive and drink';
do we, the Church, do the same in a spiritual sense?
The guards mount road blocks
to safeguard foolish drivers and pedestrians;
do we, the Church, do the same in a spiritual sense?
Or do we pass by mangled souls in tortured lives?
Have we become immune to suicides and broken homes
and shattered dreams and false gods?
Have we failed to put up barriers
warning where the steep cliffs are
that plunge into spiritual darkness?
Have we failed to put traffic lights
at the intersection of youthful hormones?
Have we created quiet oases and lay-bys
where the weary traveller can rest, spiritually?
Or do we really care when souls lie mangled
on the road to heaven or hell,
or do we really believe enough to weep?
We do care!
But because our signs are constantly being broken
or taken away and replaced by different signs,
by a world going in a different direction,
we are in danger of feeling it is useless
to put up Christian traffic-lights any more.
And we are tempted to give up trying to win their hearts for
    Christ,
and instead preach God's mercy and compassion
when they are dead.

The lapsed teenager/rebel speaks

Get up for Mass!
Say your prayers!
Did you go to confession?
God is watching you!
Don't come home pregnant!
Take that provocative dress off you.
We'll say the Rosary now.
If I catch you drinking!
Never mind what your pals say.

That's all I seemed to hear you say.
I know you meant well
and that you lived up to what you believed
but I couldn't match your expectations.
That's what I lived for,
to meet your expectations,
the huge moral expectations you had
and the rules that were laid down
by you and the Church, promising –
'The truth will make you free'.
We weren't free.

I wanted to be free from you,
from God watching me to punish me.
What a surprise I got, like being freed from prison,
the day we had the row and I left home
and broke the rules and didn't go to Mass
and lived with my boyfriend
and found I wasn't punished,
that I was free
to make up my own rules.
And you ask me am I happy?
I'm free, isn't that enough?
I'm sure I'll find happiness some day,
as you would say, 'please God!'

The parent of a suicide victim speaks

You buried him.
I expected nice words
that would console,
but the words you spoke were hard.
Can I forgive you?
You said that this was not the way,
that this was not a solution to whatever problem
drove a young man to take his own life.
My heart knew that. It was inconsolable.
Can I forgive you?
I know it was intended for the others,
the hundreds who came to his removal,
who turned up at the solemn requiem
with sweet prayers and floral tributes and well-meaning
    gestures.
'This is not the way to end one's story.'
Can I forgive you?
'This is the third coffin we have walked beside
to the graveyard in Drumreana beyond,
with young men carrying white willow wands
to signify young life cut off in its prime.'
Your words stung me to the heart.
Can I forgive you?
Yes.... The crowds had grown.
Each funeral seemed to glorify the 'cause',
while you remarked that Willie Joe,
who died after a long illness from natural causes,
had only two cars accompanying him at his burial.
How I wish my son had such a death and funeral.
Can I forgive you
for not saying these words at the *first* suicide?
If you had, perhaps my son
would be alive now!
O God, have mercy!

A traveller speaks

My mother was from Limerick
and my Father was from Clare
– both were of the travelling class.
Once we were called 'tinkers'.
We're still called that
behind our backs
and sometimes treated as such
to our face.
You say we have 'chips' on our shoulders,
that we're bleeding the welfare state.
When we'd call to your home you'd not be at home.
That's what the girl was told to say
but we'd see you behind the curtain.
When I'd say that the priests
were supposed to give us charity
you'd get mad.
Then I'd be afraid.
'Twas unlucky to make a priest mad.
As I said, my mother was from Limerick
and my father was from Clare.
There are decent people there, not like here.
They'd never see you stuck.
When you do appear
you send us to the V de P.
They give us nothing.
They say we steal.
You didn't stand up for us
when we got a house in the estate.
Only for Sister Kathleen we'd have to go back to Clare.
She seems to care.
I'm only asking you to listen.

This group came last.
Its members differed
with the Church
in doctrinal matters
and other issues,
both past and present.
Can doctrine be compromised
in reconciliation?

A married couple – contraceptives

I came to you and explained our situation
– it was fully twenty years after *Humanae Vitae* –
that if my wife got pregnant again
there was danger, the doctor said,
that her health would suffer greatly,
and even death was mentioned.
We are a God-fearing couple with five children,
five healthy children, thank God
– the last one caused the above complication.
The doctor advised my wife to go on the pill,
and when I mentioned this to you in confession
you hesitated,
and asked had we tried the Billings method.
We went to the Family Centre and learned it.
But my wife was worried
that in spite of all the charting and testing
she would still get pregnant
and her health would suffer
and the loss would be the family's.
You asked us what was the alternative,
and when I said contraceptives you asked 'which ones?'
You listed them out
– the pill, condoms, the diaphragm
coil, vasectomy, tubal ligation,
and if they failed, abortion.
We were totally and utterly
against abortion.
You gave us literature on each of them
which pointed out the implications
both morally and medically,
and we were as confused as ever.
We came back to you for guidance
and you told us that, in the end,
we had to make the decision.
We never had intercourse since.
My friends say that the Church has caused
an appalling situation with *Humanae Vitae*.

The priest/confessor replies

Yes! I remember the situation
and so many other instances in confessions
when you and so many conscientious persons
would confess and seek direction about difficult circumstances.
Questions about taxation and family planning
really made the toes turn up in the confessional.
How I wished that *Humanae Vitae* had never existed!
It would have been easier for everyone, including the Pope,
if he had followed the advice of some on the commission
and hadn't made the crucial statement:
'every act of intercourse must be open to life'.
Some of my colleagues had no problems.
They gave liberal interpretations and were very popular.
I wished I could find it that simple.
I too had a conscience to follow,
which in the words of Shakespeare, 'makes cowards of us all'.
When I'd hear 'Father we're, using contraceptives'
or 'Father, I'm not paying all my taxes',
I'd not enquire about restitution or purpose of amendment
unless the penitent asked me for some direction.
I agreed with you and Mary
that another child seemed not to be God's providence,
and we went through each method conscientiously:
the pill – now an abortifacient since it affected progesterone;
the coil and IUD – clearly abortifacients, which both of
you said were morally reprehensible;
The diaphragm and the condom – unsafe even if they were
morally acceptable.
There was Billings but you were nervous about its usage,
even if it was used with condoms to protect against failures.
There was vasectomy and tubal ligation,
which at that time were thought to be totally reliable.
There was also abstinence – total abstinence
with the grace of God assisting.
Then it was a question of conscience, for both you and Mary.
You eventually opted for total abstinence.
Perhaps it would not have been my decision
had I been in your situation.
But that is where the conscience (informed) is absolute.
In a way, *Humanae Vitae* was not only about contraceptives,
it was also about conscience
as arbitrator of our decisions.

A mixed marriage –
ne temere

ne temere

Your mother was shocked.
Mine was appalled.
A Catholic in ours.
A Protestant in yours.
Mothers-in-law can be awkward.
So can Mother Church.

ne temere

Are we baptised in Christ or not?
Are we equal before God or not?
Are we children beloved of the Father or not?
Does Christ walk on one pilgrim road
and not the other?

ne temere

'Are you Catholic or Protestant?'
Is that what we will be asked at Judgement?
'Did you bring up your children Catholic or Protestant?'
Won't it be:
'Were you truly Christian' and
'Did you help your children be truly Christian?'
In what part of the Judgement,
in what part of the cross-examination,
in what part of circumstantial evidence
will it be asked
whether you were Catholic or Protestant
or Presbyterian?

ne temere

A reflection on the theme

I watched a boat
sunk in the mud
beside a pier in Ramelton.
Its ribs were sticking out
from the slime-green sand
and I conjured up a time
when craftsmen shaped the oak
and built a study craft
that sailed the open sea
without fear.

ne temere

But times have changed
and nowadays
crafts need to be different.
Each age has to cope as best it can
with the sea and surf and wind and tide
of life.
We tried to keep the ship afloat.
We sailed and failed
to see the way clearly
because of a mist at sea
and therefore we were cautious of rocks.

ne temere

The mist of centuries is rising now
and we must shape a new craft in Christ
that in the dawn
will be fit to face
a turbulent sea.

ne temere

'Do not be afraid.
Am I not with you!'

Second unions and Communions

First Communion
Veils
White dresses
Parents present
Go to altar
Tongue or hand
Cross my arms
Bow my head
Receive a blessing
Return to seat
Hear her prayer
'Fáilte Romhat
a Íosa dhil!
Fáilte romhat!'
Her heart, his home.

I'm not worthy!
Living in sin!
Previously married!
A source of scandal!
Bad example!
Angry!

On this special day
this child of God,
with Him in deep communion,
could not be a child of ours.
Who makes such laws?

A reflection
on the theme

Previously married
Bad example
Source of scandal
Not worthy
Who is?
Your heart his home?
Who knows?

God does,
and he alone,
and you can know too
if your heart can truly say
'Fáilte Romhat,
Fáilte Romhat
A Íosa Dhil'
and he leaves his peace.

Veils
White dresses
Tongue or hand
– these are only outward dressings.
God knows the heart.
Communion!

While we are here on earth
the yardstick by which we measure
the Mystery
is inserted in its dark waters
and in the light of the refraction
we shape its laws and customs
imperfectly.

We are still pilgrims.

Abortion – the guilt you made me feel

I saw aborted foetuses in a plastic bucket
in a booklet issued by a Church group
and I was horrified, disgusted and filled with contempt
for a Church body that would allow such propaganda.

Oh! you said that it had got no imprimatur,
but it was and is being sold in many churches
together with descriptions of all the abortion methods.
What do you suppose you are trying to foster?

Yes, I had an abortion. I'll spare you the circumstances.
But I don't want to be confronted by such crudity.
You say the Church is compassionate!
Then why do you not speak of 'termination of pregnancy'
or some other terminology more in keeping with humanity?

My friend went for counselling after her abortion.
She couldn't sleep at night. She needed therapy.
It was the picture in the magazine that shocked her.
She seems to be fine now! How? I never asked her.

What if she hadn't had the counselling or gone for therapy?
Who would be to blame for her loss of sanity?
The Church and its obscene descriptions and drawings?
Not likely!
Guilt, you say, precedes forgiveness.
Is that why you show these plastic buckets –
to stir up guilt in Catholic Ireland?

If that is so, isn't it time
we got rid of all
'plastic guilt'?

A counterpoint

Yes! I was shocked when I saw
aborted foetuses in plastic buckets.
Hitherto in conversation I sometimes said 'abortion'
when I had meant to say 'adoption'
and never adverted to the chasm between them.

I used euphemisms like 'terminate the pregnancy'
and called unborn babies foetuses or zygotes
and saw abortions as operations done in hospitals.
It wasn't until I saw those plastic buckets
and read how abortions are performed
that I was shocked into action.

Yes. I've seen the book and sometimes recommend it,
not to make those who had abortions guilty
but to forewarn those who are contemplating
this final solution to their problem.

We read with utter revulsion of Hitler's 'final solution'
and see photos of Belsen and Auschwitz to prove authenticity.
In a thousand years from now or maybe only twenty
will someone not look back on photos of aborted babies
and discover what happened to 56,000,000 of them around the
    world, yearly?
And will they not wonder why no one bothered
to tell the truth of what was really happening?
I am the counsellor of the friend you referred to.
She told me I could tell her story to anyone.
She came to terms with the tragedy that happened.
'It' was no longer 'it' but a human being.
Her guilt was tempered by God's great compassion
and his mercy and forgiveness.
She claimed the child and named 'it' Francis.
A boy or a girl?
She'll know when they meet in heaven.

Green Christianity

The Boyne flowed between us.
It still does.
'We won that day!'
That is what we hear you say.
You're not listening to us
and what we have to say.

You beat your Lambeth drums.
'We won that day!'
That's what we heard them say.
You're not listening to us
and what we have to say.

You ask us a question:
'Could there be a different drummer
whom we could both hear without fear,
and learn the rhythm of His dance
echoing across the Jordan river?'

And we ask ourselves the question:
'Have we in our Church
interfered with the rhythm of His dance
through the accumulated side-steps
of history?'

Orange Christianity

The Boyne flows deep and wide.
It must always be crossed,
not once but in every generation.
Each generation must cross it.
It is the badge of our identity.
It is what makes us what we are.
It is our life and our religion.

You don't hear us.
You don't listen to us.
You only hear the beat of the *bodhrán*.
Our drums and yours
are miles apart.
They beat a different rhythm.

You ask us a question:
'Must your drums be so loud
that you cannot hear the sound
of another drummer
whom we both profess to know
and could follow together
across the Jordan River?'

And we ask ourselves the question:
'Have we, as Church,
muffled His message
with the drumsticks
of history?'

Compassion

They arrived at the appointed place
where He who bore all crosses stood,
welcoming saint and sinner with open arms.
He lifted the burden from each one's shoulder
and placed it in a circle around the Cross,
which He for us had borne.
They sat around in silence.
and as his gaze looked with love into each heart
they knew instinctively that He knew and understood
the weight and burden of the cross they carried.
He spoke in tongues but no sound came,
yet each one heard his words within the heart,
which changed the weight and texture of the cross they
    carried.
He then raised his hands and gave a blessing.
And then He gave a strange direction and a choice –
whoever wished could exchange their cross for his,
or for the cross of those who had caused them pain,
or they could embrace their own,
now transformed with compassionate love.
And if they were to travel further with him
in the peace and joy they now experienced,
they must allow his compassion to flow,
which forgave the other
and sought forgiveness for themselves.
Strange as it may seem
none of them exchanged their crosses for his
and few if any took the crosses of their afflictors.
Those who did left them down again
for they realised that they were very heavy,
that their own crosses
fitted their own shoulders best
for the rest of the journey home.

The ritual expression

Those who experienced this faith encounter
wished to express ritually
that which was happening within them.
It was springtime of the year,
and the dry clay felt fresh beneath their feet.
Those who wished for reconciliation removed their shoes,
for, whether they were the hurt or the hurting, they were
    penitents.
They formed a large circle around the one
who had been appointed as representative of themselves
and of Christ, present but invisible, except to the eyes of faith.
The others moved away.
Some sat in silence on sullen rocks
while others scoffed scornfully from adjacent fields.
The representative invited those circled to bend low
and take a handful of clay from beneath their feet
and hold it tightly in their clenched fists.
He spoke at length about the grasping nature of our being
and how reluctant we were even to let go of 'hurt'.
He invited them to let their fingers open slowly
so that the clay slipped gracefully to the earth,
as if letting go of the hurt that they were nurturing.
Then, spontaneously, they dropped to their knees
and with their index fingers, now free to write,
they traced the symbols of their own sins in the clay.
There arose a muffled cry of agony and grief,
calling on God's mercy and forgiveness,
for they experienced, in that blessed moment of grace,
the anguish of the damned and the effects of sin
in the inner recesses of their inmost being.
It was only a moment, a fleeting second, but it seemed an
    eternity.
Justice and Mercy met that day and embraced,
and there was Peace.
The representative asked them to rise
and ask forgiveness from those whom they had hurt most.
In doing so, their feet destroyed the sin symbols in the clay
and their sins no longer appeared upon the earth.
He raised his hand and in the name of the Triune God
pronounced that their sins had disappeared in heaven too,
and the Spirit came upon them as a proof.
Spontaneously, they turned around with outstretched hands
and invited those who sat on sullen rocks

or who scoffed and scorned from adjacent fields
to join with them and share the peace they had.
Some did and some did not.
And they saw the Virgin Mother there,
and she was crying.
They turned towards the centre once again,
and each received a tiny sapling of a yew
to plant in the fertile clay beneath their feet.
In years to come these grew into a mighty grove,
which outlived and outgrew a millennium or more,
a symbol of a momentous moment in a momentous day
to all who subsequently passed that way.
They set out on pilgrimage again
and, as their penance, took the cross they carried
and walked joyfully with Christ.

A new beginning

For those who set out again with Christ
and travelled on the pilgrim road with him,
there came a new understanding
that all pilgrims
are wounded and wounding creatures
and need constant healing
and forgiveness.
And the source of this healing
and forgiveness
is the Lamb
who takes away
the sins of the world
and gives us peace.
With this understanding
there came a new compassion.
And with the compassion
came a realisation
that we are not knights or gallant crusaders
riding up to the doors of heaven.
Ah! No! We are but humble pilgrims supporting one another
along the road trod by Him
who was hurt but who never wounded
except for healing.
And the Spirit will lead us to the portals of heaven
on whose doors are written large:
'Welcome home, and forgiveness
to all who, in turn, have forgiven others'.

A 'no' beginning

There is another road into the new millennium,
which stretches on and on,
for those who will not let go of their bitter hurt.
Along the road the wounded pilgrims
will tell their bitter stories to each other,
of unredeemed hurt and anger.
And they will become deep companions
on the bitter road that has no ending.
And the tragedy will be all the greater
in that, at the end of the next millennium
or the next century,
or even the next generation,
when we will set down to pause again
on our pilgrim journey,
some of these victims
will have become perpetrators,
just as, in our own pause now,
some of the criminals of today
were the victims of yesterday.
And so the bitter journey will go on and on
gathering more fellow pilgrims on the way
millennium after millennium after millennium
on the unforgiving road of pain.
Who would have thought that Kosovo
dates back to the Crusades,
or that Omagh is an echo of the Boyne?
And the road goes on and on,
stretching up and out and beyond,
never ending, never coming home
to the door on whose portals are written
the healing words of the Father:
'Welcome home, and forgiveness
to all who, in turn, have forgiven others'.

The pilgrim road ahead

And shall we walk a pilgrim road as a Church
where there will be no more sin or scandals,
a Church of perfect peace and harmony,
a Church of perfect charity?
Not likely!
For Christ came not to call the just,
but the sinners,
and it seems he will continue to do so
again and again into the millennium.
Some will become saints,
and others will still be sinners,
and some will be saints today
and sinners tomorrow,
and vice versa.
The Church as institution
will continue to be a Church,
a Church, guided by the Spirit,
of saints and sinners,
a scandal to those within it who never falter.
And in spite of its best efforts
it will have to call again and again
on the mercy of our Father,
for we are His sinful children, whom He loves
– pilgrims in search of wholeness.